LILLENAS® DRAMA

I0884664

Patriotic Program Builder

Creative Resources for Program Directors

Compiled by

Kimberly R. Messer

Lillenas® PUBLISHING COMPANY

KANSAS CITY, MO 64141

Questions? Please write or call:
Lillenas Publishing Company
Drama Resources
P. O. Box 419527
Kansas City, MO 64141
Phone: 816-931-1900 • Fax: 816-412-8390
E-mail: drama@lillenas.com
Web Site: www.lillenasdrama.com

Cover design: Michael Walsh

Contents

Preschool Recitations

Little Soldier

I'm just a little soldier. *(Stands straight with arms to side)*
My mom thinks I am cute! *(Cups hand to mouth as if whispering)*
But I am here today, *(Points to self)*
To give you a big salute! *(Salutes audience)*

Enelle Eder

God Made

(For one or several children)

God made the sun *(move hands in a big circle)*
To light the day.
He made the moon, *(make fingers into fist, putting both hands together)*
A nighttime ray.
God made the stars *(point upwards)*
All twinkly and bright. *(Wiggle fingers)*
He made the wind *(blow softly)*
That flies our flag just right. *(Move hand as if waving a flag)*
God made me *(point to self)* in a special way,
So I will pray *(fold hands as praying)* on this patriotic holiday!

Wanda E. Brunstetter

Happy Birthday

We have come here to say,
Happy birthday, U.S.A.

Rebecca K. Grosenbach

Freedom, Freedom, Let Us Sing!

(Sung to the tune, "Twinkle, Twinkle, Little Star")

Freedom, freedom, let us sing
Of our nation's history
Will you celebrate with us?
Come and join us, do not fuss.
Freedom, freedom, may it be
Full of life and liberty.

Amy Spence

Three Cheers

(Children may pull small flags out from behind their backs and wave them at end.)

Bang the drum, ring the bell
Young and old give a yell!
Let's all say, hip, hip, horray!
Wave the flag! U.S.A.!

Rebecca K. Grosenbach

Proud Flags

(Each child has a small flag to wave.)

We raise our flags,
Red, white, and blue
We wave them high,
We're proud, aren't you?

Debbie Salter Goodwin

We Are Here to Celebrate

(Sung to the tune
"London Bridge Is Falling Down")

We are here to celebrate,
  Celebrate,
  Celebrate.
We are here to celebrate,
  In-de-pendence!

Come and join us, won't you all,
  Won't you all,
  Won't you all.
Come and join us, celebrate
  In-de-pendence!

Amy Spence

Wave the Flag

Wave the flag, Old Glory,
Wave the flag today.
Wave the flag, Old Glory,
And don't forget to pray.

Wave the flag, Old Glory,
Wave the flag today.
Wave the flag, Old Glory,
Read the Bible and obey.

Wave the flag, Old Glory,
Wave the flag today.
Wave the flag, Old Glory,
Hip, hip, hooray!

Wanda E. Brunstetter

I Love My Country

May God bless America,
Land of the free.
I love my country
It's where I want to be.

Margaret Primrose

Recitations for Ages 5 to 7

Remembering

Papaw, why is there a tear in your
eye?
Why are you so sad today?
What makes your heart so heavy?
Can I help take that pain away?

Papaw, why do you salute the
soldiers
As they go marching by?
Is it the memories of another day
That brings the tears to your eyes?

Papaw, are these soldiers
Like the ones that you once knew?
Do they remind you of others
When you were twenty-two?

Robert E. Snodgrass

I Tip My Hat

(Each CHILD *wears a red, white or blue patriotic hat.)*

CHILD 1: I tip my hat to freedom. *(Tips hat up.)*
CHILD 2: I tip my hat to thee. *(Tips hat toward audience.)*
CHILD 3: I tip my hat to thank the Lord.
For priceless liberty.
(Tips hat upward, looking to heaven)

Amy Spence

Parade on the 4th

The street's lined with red, white,
and blue—
It's wonderful to see.
My heart fills up with pride and
love.
America's for me!

Janet Lombard

One of a Kind

(Each CHILD *holds a small personal flag, which he or she holds up and waves when he or she speaks.)*

CHILD 1: I'm waving my flag for freedom.
CHILD 2: I'll wave my flag each day.
CHILD 3: I'm waving my flag for justice.
CHILD 4: Mine for the American way.
ALL *(waving flags):*
We'll wave our flags together.
We'll wave them anytime
Just to show we love our land;
It's truly one of a kind.

Amy Spence

A Man in Uniform

(May be recited by a group of girls looking at a boy, or a group of boys dressed in military uniform costume, or an adult in a real uniform.)

We love a man in uniform.
He looks his very best.
Every button in its place,
His creases freshly pressed.
But more than that we love the men
And women who risked all.
Who bravely wore these uniforms
When America gave the call.
ONE GIRL: Will all the men and women who have served in our military please stand so we may thank you with a round of applause?

Rebecca K. Grosenbach

We're Soldiers

(First four lines delivered by eight children in two lines of four children each, standing two deep, marching to center of stage in formation as they speak.)

Left! Right! Left! Right!
Down the street we go.
Left! Right! Left! Right!
Marching row by row.

(Second four lines delivered as four children turn right, four turn left to form a straight line.)

We don't have guns and bullets.
We have the Spirit's sword. *(Raise Bibles)*
We're not in the U.S. Army.
We're soldiers of the Lord.
Hallelujah!

Margaret Primrose

Day Welcome

Welcome to our program
On this patriotic day.
Let's praise the Lord together
For the U. S. of A.

Amy Spence

Night Welcome

Welcome to our program
On this patriotic night.
Let's thank the Lord together
For all of freedom's rights.

Amy Spence

The 4th of July

Hamburgers and hot dogs,
And baseball in the sun,
Camping, boating, swimming,
More patriotic fun.
Picnics, games, parades,
And fireworks in the sky.
Happy celebrating!
It's the 4th of July!

Dorothy Heibel

Let's Remember July 4th

(Sung to the tune
"Take Me Out to the Ball Game.")

Let's remember July 4th.
Let's remember this day.
Stand to your feet and clap your hands.
Please stand up and show us you can.

For it's free . . . free . . . freedom
We cel-e-brate;
If you don't care it's a shame.
'Cause we won't stop singing the praise,
Of this joy-ous day.

Amy Spence

Raise a Flag for Liberty

Props:

Penalty flag
Checkered race flag
Car sales flag
Military flag
American flag

CHILD 1 *(wearing a referee shirt and holding a penalty flag):* Some raise a flag to ref a game.

CHILD 2 *(holds a checkered flag as if ready to start a race):* Some raise a flag to race.

CHILD 3 & 4 *(holding a large banner-type flag advertising a retail store or restaurant):* Some raise a flag to show their name.

CHILD 5 *(wearing a military hat and holding a military flag):* Some raise a flag at base.

CHILD 6 *(with a large American flag):*
But I raise a flag to show the world
That I am proud to be
Living in America,
The land of liberty.

Debbie Salter Goodwin

My Prayer for Daddy

I miss my daddy, Jesus;
I miss him every day.
I know he loves his country . . .
That's why he's far away.

I pray you'll bless my daddy,
And keep him in your care.
I know that you can do it
Because you're everywhere.

Margaret Primrose

God's Great Hand

I stand taller when the flag goes by.
I am so proud as I watch it fly.
The flag waves boldly over our land,
One nation under God's great hand.

Robert E. Snodgrass

I Like the 4th of July

CHILD 1: I like grilling hot dogs
And splashing in a pool.
I like summer vacation
When I don't have to go to school.
CHILD 2: I like marching bands
And decorated floats.
I like ice-cream parties
And cruising the lake in a boat.
CHILD 3: The red and gold of a sunset
Compare to a lullaby,
But I also like the fireworks
That color the evening sky.
CHILD 4: The 4th of July is special
In a land where pilgrims trod,
Where church bells ring each Sunday
And we're free to worship God.

Margaret Primrose

An Armed Forces "Thank You"

(Children may hold up large handmade thank-you cards.)

Thank you to our Navy
For what you do each day.
Thank you to our Army
Who fight for the U.S.A.

And how about our Air Force
Who fly courageously?
Thanks a lot to our Marines
Who protect us fearlessly.

Don't forget the Coast Guard
Who rescue those in need.
A great big thanks to all of you
For planting freedom's seed.

Amy Spence

Recitations for Ages 8 to 10

The Flag

(Each CHILD *holds a banner that says "FLAG" across the top with a picture of the American flag below. Reveal one letter at a time with each speaker.)*

CHILD 1: **F** Is for the freedom
Our soldiers fought to win.
Their loyalty was tested
Time and time again.

CHILD 2: **L** Represents their love
For country, God and kin.
So off they march to battle.
Sometimes they could not win.

CHILD 3: **A** Stands for America,
A warm and welcome place
Who takes in weary travelers,
From every land and race.

CHILD 4: **G** Stands for our God,
The one who guides the hand
Of those who unselfishly protect
Their precious native land.

ALL: Our flag stands for freedom.
It's the reason that men fight.
They proudly honor and protect
The blue, the red, the white.

Enelle Eder

Freedom's Colors

Our flag is made up
Of the red, white, and blue.
We give honor today
To where it is due.

Red is for valor,
The strong and the brave
White means purity,
Long may she wave.

Blue's for vigilance,
Careful, watchful eye.
Our flag of freedom,
Long may she fly.

Amy Spence

The Big Idea

It's something that's worth fighting for,
But something you can't see.
America was built on this–
It's called equality.

Janet Lombard

Remembering Grandma

I had a special grandma
Who used to read to me.
Her house was always quiet
And as neat as it could be.

I like her chocolate cookies,
And I like her apple pie.
I was very, very sad
When I heard that she might die.

I cried when she went to heaven,
But why should I be sad?
I know that she is happy,
And that helps to make me glad.

Sometimes we go to her grave
To leave some flowers there.
Then we thank the Lord for
Grandma
As we bow our heads in prayer.

Margaret Primrose

God's Rainbow

CHILD 1 *(holding or pointing to an American flag):*
See the colors of our flag
The red and white and
blue
Reminding us how
freedom
Is as strong as me and you.

CHILD 2 *(holding a white sign with the word "Purity" written on it):*
White stands for the purity
It takes to make us strong.
Purely seeking what is
right
And shunning what is
wrong.

CHILD 3 *(holding a red sign with the word "Valor" written on it):*
Red is for the valor
It takes to keep us free;
The soldiers during
wartime
Who fought for you and
me.

CHILD 4 *(holding a blue sign with the word "Justice" written on it):*
Blue stands for the justice
That protects our basic
rights
With laws that govern all
of us
Instead of force or might.

CHILD 5 *(first three children hold up their signs again):*
And yet these colors also
speak
Of what our God has done
When He sent Jesus here to
earth,
His one and only Son.

CHILD 6 *(raise "Purity" sign again):*
White is for the purity
Of heart that God desires.
He wants to make our
hearts brand-new
And clean them with His
fire.

CHILD 7 *(raise "Valor" sign again):*
Red is for a valor
No other ever gave.
When Jesus died upon the
cross
It was for sin to save.

CHILD 8 *(raise "Justice" sign again):*
And who is any better
judge
Than God who never fails
To share the truth with all
of us,
His judgment never pales.

CHILD 9: "My Country 'Tis of Thee,"
we sing
And colors say it too.
We celebrate God's
rainbow in
The red, the white, and
blue. *(Raise all signs.)*

Debbie Salter Goodwin

God Bless Our Soldiers

(Names and type of services may be changed.)

I have an Uncle Gregory
Who's far across the sea.
He's a pilot in the Air Force
And he means a lot to me.

Each night before I sleep,
I kneel and say a prayer,
"Lord, bless my Uncle Gregory
And keep him in your care."

"Please bless our other soldiers.
They need protection too.
Although I do not know them,
They mean a lot to you."

Margaret Primrose

Remember When

September 11th will always be
A day to remember when
Our nation stood in silence
As we saw the hate of men.

Many perished on that day,
Forever in our hearts they'll be.
I thank the Lord, despite this act
We're bound in unity.

Amy Spence

Adult Recitations

A Patriotic Prayer

Long may our country's flag
Proudly wave
Over our nation
So strong and brave.
Long may our hearts beat
With trust and pride
As we ask God, the Father
To be our loving guide.

Dorothy Heibel

How I Remember 9-11

My bus had taken a detour.
I was late for my appointment that day.
The doctor was not on schedule.
The sky had begun to gray.

I hurried toward the bus stop
To wait alone on the street.
I feared the riding with people
I might not like to meet.

I passed drivers waiting for gas
Although the price had soared.
Of course, I would have paid it too
If I hadn't wrecked my Ford.

On the bus was an anti-American
Who said things I didn't like.
My thoughts were on the last few blocks
That I soon would have to hike.

I prayed as I hurried home
To a building with unlighted stairs.
Though dinner might be by candlelight
I continued with my prayers.

I shuddered when I watched the replays
Of our country's crumbling towers,
And marveled at the courage
Of those who had suffered there for hours.

My pastor called to invite me
To go to the church for prayer.
We knelt and asked for guidance
For a nation in despair.

Thank God, He is still in control,
And thank God, He will always be
Ready, willing and able
To hear each earnest plea.

Margaret Primrose

Memorial Day

On Memorial Day we honor
All the people who have died
To keep our country safe,
Our freedom to provide.

They did not refuse to go
When they heard their country call,
But proudly faced the task,
And gave America their all.

So on this special day
We pause to give their due
To the noble, valiant souls
Who defended the red, white, and blue!

Enelle Eder

Dear God

Grant us wisdom,
Grant us courage,
Grant us the end of strife.
May we conquer death
And accept the Way
To a safer, more peaceful life!

Dorothy Heibel

If My People Will Pray

(May be used as a transition between music or over an introduction to a song.)

Robert E. Lee delivered this eloquent and profound statement in 1864. It is as true and vital today as it was then.

> "Knowing that intercessory prayer is our mightiest weapon and the uppermost call for all Christians today, I pleadingly urge our people everywhere to pray. Believing that prayer is the greatest contribution that our people can make in this critical hour, I humbly urge that we take time to pray . . . to really pray. Let us pray for our children, our youth, our aged, our pastors, our homes. Let us pray for our nation. Let us pray for those who have never known Jesus Christ and redeeming love, for moral forces everywhere and for our national leaders. Let prayer be our passion. Let prayer be our practice."

God, our Father, even more eloquently proclaims: "If my people, which are called by my name, shall humble themselves, and pray, and seek my face, and turn from their wicked ways; then will I hear from heaven, and will forgive their sin, and will heal their land." (2 Chronicles 7:14, KJV)

Derric Johnson

Forgiveness

A prayer that in these dangerous
    days
Of battle, war, and strife,
We may take time to remember
The way Christ gave up His life.
Even on the cross His love
Remained steadfast and true.
He said, "Father, forgive them
For they know not what they do!"
Our Lord lay down His precious life
Forgiving you and me,
So that we might share His glory
And live eternally.

Dorothy Heibel

Because

Because they couldn't own their
    land,
  Or keep a little store . . .
Because their faith was not allowed
  And their hearts yearned for
    more . . .
Because the U.S. still means hope,
  Though it's not perfect here . . .
Somehow, they come; they hear the
    call
  Of Freedom ringing clear.

Janet Lombard

A Prayer for Our Nation

Lord, help our nation
To always work for peace,
To keep earth's produce plentiful
Its bounty to increase,
So that we may ever share
With those who are in need.
Keep us following You, Lord,
In prayer and word and deed!

Dorothy Heibel

If God Be for Us

(May be used as a transition between music or over the introduction to a song.)

We dare not rely on our own strength for security and stability. In the long run it is not the caliber of a nation's guns that makes it strong and secure . . . it is the caliber of the men behind the guns. Our defense is not the force of our arms but the moral fiber of our citizens; and the quality of that fiber can be measured by how much we rely upon God for strength and guidance. "Without God there is no prompting of the conscience; without God there is a coarsening of the society; without God democracy will not and can not long endure. If we ever forget that we are one nation under God, then we will be a nation gone under."

Derric Johnson with Quote Spoken by Ronald Reagan

Responsive Reading

4th of July

LEADER: Picnics, parades, and sparklers,
Marching bands and more!
PEOPLE: Gathering with our family
To watch fireworks galore!
LEADER: Celebrating independence
From the rule of England's hand.
PEOPLE: Remembering the freedoms
That make our country grand.
LEADER: God gave our founding fathers
Wisdom to build a strong foundation.
To stand against all prejudice
And create a Christian nation.
PEOPLE: We are a people truly blessed,
So let's rise our flags up high
ALL: For the freedoms we enjoy
On this, the 4th of July!

Enelle Eder

Story

The Story of "In Flanders Fields"

by Rebecca K. Grosenbach

Production Notes: Many people's inclination is to read poetry "line by line," reading each line as a separate phrase. The more accurate method of reading poetry is to follow the punctuation. This gives a more fluid, natural expression to the thoughts of the poem. For instance, read "In Flanders Fields" as if it were written in paragraphs. Here is one example of how to break the phrases:

In Flanders fields the poppies blow between the crosses,
Row on row,
That mark our place.
And in the sky the larks,
Still bravely singing,
Fly scarce heard amid the guns below.
We are the Dead.
Short days ago we lived,
felt dawn,
saw sunset glow,
loved and were loved,
And now we lie in Flanders fields.

Take up our quarrel with the foe;
To you from failing hands we throw the torch;
Be yours to hold it high.
If ye break faith with us who die we shall not sleep
Though poppies grow in Flanders fields.

During World War I, a poem called "In Flanders Fields" voiced the heartbreak of those who had lost loved ones in the conflict, and the importance of completing the task to which those soldiers sacrificed their lives.

The poem was written by John McCrae, a Canadian physician. When World War I broke out, McCrae was sent to Belgium as a field surgeon in the Canadian artillery. He was in charge of a field hospital during the second Battle of Ypres [e-pray] in 1915. McCrae's friend, Alexis Helmer, was killed in the battle, and his burial inspired the poem. In 1918, while still serving in the field hospital, McCrae caught pneumonia and meningitis, and died.

Flanders is a region in northern Belgium. The poppies referred to in the poem grew in profusion in the fields where war casualties had been buried. Poppies have since become a symbol of remembrance for fallen soldiers. The poem reads:

In Flanders fields the poppies blow
Between the crosses, row on row,
That mark our place; and in the sky
The larks, still bravely singing, fly
Scarce heard amid the guns below.
We are the Dead. Short days ago
We lived, felt dawn, saw sunset glow,
Loved, and were loved, and now we lie
In Flanders fields.

Take up our quarrel with the foe:
To you from failing hands we throw
The torch; be yours to hold it high.
If ye break faith with us who die
We shall not sleep, though poppies grow
In Flanders fields.

Readers Theatre

Freedom and Responsibility

by Debbie Salter Goodwin

*(*READER 2 *interrupts* READER 1 *with side comments, obviously focused on the wrong issues. Use different readers for scriptures to increase participation.)*

READER 1: Today we celebrate freedom . . .

READER 2: Yeah! Freedom!

READER 1: We live in a country that believes everyone should be free.

READER 2: Yeah! Everyone!

READER 1: We believe in freedom of speech,

READER 2: Tell it like it is! Tell us how you feel!

READER 1: Freedom to worship,

READER 2: Any way you want!

READER 1: Freedom to life, liberty, and the pursuit of happiness.

READER 2: Yeah! Especially happiness!

READER 1: But these freedoms come with responsibilities.

READER 2: They do?

READER 1: Yes, they do!

READER 2: What kind of responsibility?

READER 1: The responsibility to speak the truth in love.

READER 3: 1 Corinthians 2:13, "This is what we speak, not in words taught us by human wisdom but in words taught by the Spirit, expressing spiritual truths in spiritual words."

READER 2: Oh!

READER 1: The responsibility to use our worship according to God's desires.

READER 4: Romans 12:1, "Therefore, I urge you, brothers, in view of God's mercy, to offer your bodies as living sacrifices, holy and pleasing to God—this is your spiritual act of worship."

READER 2: Our whole body, huh?

READER 1: The responsibility to live life the way that God, the Creator of life, designed it:

READER 5: Mark 8:35, "For whoever wants to save his life will lose it, but whoever loses his life for me and for the gospel will save it."

READER 2: Wow! That's a lot of responsibility.

READER 1: No, that's a lot of freedom.

The Signers

by Rebecca K. Grosenbach

(This piece can be done as a four person readers theatre or with the readers memorizing their parts. It could also be done with fewer persons by redividing the parts, by one person as a monologue.)

READER 1: "We hold these Truths to be self-evident, that all Men are created equal . . .

READERS 1 & 2: that they are endowed by their Creator with certain unalienable Rights, that among these are

READERS 1, 2, & 3: Life, Liberty, and the Pursuit of Happiness."

READER 4: These famous words from the Declaration of Independence were penned by Thomas Jefferson, Virginian delegate to the Continental Congress.

READER 2: Jefferson was one of 16 lawyers to sign the Declaration.

READER 3: The list also included 13 judges.

READER 4: The other half of the 58 signers were not of a legal or political background.

READER 1: There were four physicians,

READER 3: Ten farmers and ten merchants,

READER 2: A publisher, and an author.

READER 4: A soldier, an iron master, and two educators.

READER 1: Roger Sherman from Connecticut identified himself as a cobbler, surveyor, and lawyer.

READER 2: Many of the signers were well educated. William Ellery graduated from Harvard at age 15.

READER 3: Others had little or no formal educations.

READERS 1 & 2: Two men, John Adams and Samuel Adams, were cousins.

READER 4: Benjamin Franklin was the oldest at 70.

READER 3: Edward Rutledge, the youngest, was only 26.

READER 2: These men, while varied in age, education, and occupation, displayed a single mind and heart in signing the Declaration of Independence.

READER 1: Their actions displayed a rare courage; signing the Declaration could have been perceived as an act of treason against the King of England.

READER 4: Seven of the men had been born in Great Britain yet they eagerly sided with the Revolution.

READER 3: Each man was willing to die to secure our nation's independence.

READER 1: Their sacrifice and service did not end with the signing of the Declaration.

READER 3: Several men lost vast fortunes during the course of the Revolutionary War.

READER 2: Four were taken prisoner.

READER 4: Thirteen of these great men went on to become governors of their states.

READER 1: Three became U.S. Vice Presidents.

READER 3: Two, John Adams and Thomas Jefferson, went on to become Presidents. These two men died on the same day, July 4, 1826, fifty years after signing the Declaration.

READER 2: Each man who loaned his name to this document sided with Thomas Jefferson when he wrote,

ALL: "for the support of this declaration, with a firm Reliance on the Protection of divine Providence, we mutually pledge to each other our lives, our Fortunes, and our sacred Honor."

Original Freedom

A readers theatre reminder that freedom is God's original idea.

by Debbie Salter Goodwin

Scriptures in order of occurrence: Genesis 2:16-17, 3:6; 2 Peter 2:19*b;* Galatians 5:13*a;* Romans 6:20*a*, 22*a*, 8:2; 1 Corinthians 8:9; Galatians 5:1*b;* Hebrews 13:5*a;* James 1:25*a;* John 8:32; 2 Corinthians 3:17*b;* Romans 6:22; 1 Peter 2:16; John 8:36.

READER 1: And the LORD God commanded . . .

READER 2: You are free to eat from any tree in the garden;

READER 1: Except . . .

READER 2: you must not eat from the tree of the knowledge of good and evil, for when you eat of it you will surely die.

READER 1: When the woman saw that the fruit of the tree was good . . . and pleasing to the eye, . . . She took . . . and ate it. *(Pantomimes the action.)*

READER 2: Man . . .

READER 1: Or woman . . .

READER 2: Is slave to whatever has mastered him.

READER 1: But you . . . were called to be free.

READER 2: You were slaves to sin.

READER 1: But now . . . you have been set free from sin.

READER 2: Christ Jesus has set you free from the law of sin and death.

READER 1: Be careful, however, that the exercise of your freedom does not become a stumbling block to the weak.

READER 2: Do not let yourselves be burdened again by a yoke of slavery.

READER 1: Keep your lives free from the love of money.

READER 2: Be content with what you have.

READER 1: Look intently into the perfect law that gives freedom.

READER 2: Then you will know the truth,

READER 1: And the truth will set you free.

READER 2: Where the Spirit of the Lord is, there is freedom.

READER 1: You have been set free from sin . . .

READER 2: To become slaves to God;

READER 1: The result is eternal life.

READER 2: Live as free men and women.

READER 1: Live as servants of God.

READER 2: Remember,

READER 1: If the Son sets you free . . .

READERS 1 & 2: You will be free indeed.

Monologues

Taps

by Judy Gertach

Scripture: 1 Corinthians 14:8; 1 Corinthians 15:52

Themes: Patriotic; serving God and country; "Taps" tribute; honoring the dead of America's military

Tone: Serious

Cast:

SEAN—A man in his late 50s

Props:

Military uniform
Bugle

Synopsis: A veteran of the United States Army Field Band, who now makes his living as a professional musician, tells how he continues to serve his country as a bugler who is called upon regularly to play "Taps" for military funerals. Sean recounts the story of one experience in particular when the 24-note melody became much more to him than a bugle call to honor the dead soldier.

Running Time: 5 minutes. (If "Taps" included, 6 minutes.)

(If the actor is not a real bugler who can sound "Taps," play a recorded version of the call before the actor enters the stage and the monologue begins. If the actor can play, have him enter the stage, stand slightly off to one side, and sound the "Taps" before speaking. He should start walking toward SC as he begins to speak; deliver with emotion.)

SEAN: Those notes. Those 24 notes. The stirring, yet melancholy sound of that famous bugle call known simply as "Taps." I've probably sounded that call a thousand times in my life. *(Stops CS)*

Hi . . . my name is Sean. I'm a professional musician in the Baltimore area. I began my career playing trumpet in the United States Army Field Band when I was a young man in my 20s. For the next 30 years I served my country as a member of the Field Band, playing concerts all around the globe. As musical ambassadors for the Army, it was our job to keep the will of the American people behind the armed forces.

During our travels, I met a lot of interesting people and made a few new friends. For the most part, we never felt like we were in any danger. But there was one tour, about 15 years into my career, that led me down a path that I never expected to take—a dark road where death stood before me with utmost certainty. During one of our concert stops in India, I contracted a serious virus. I spent three weeks in a hospital there, too sick to be moved. The band, of course, had to go on without me. An Army chaplain, who was stationed at an American military base in Bombay, was summoned to attend me. His name was Keith. He told me that he'd heard me play at the concert and that I'd better get well quick so I could play again.

There was something special about Keith. He was genuine; his prayers were from the heart. He had a great sense of humor; and he really cared. And it was Keith who introduced me to Jesus Christ.

During that three-week stay, we became close friends. When it appeared that I wasn't going to make it, I asked Keith if he would say a few words at my funeral. He said he would, and jokingly added, "only if you'll play 'Taps' at mine."

About the middle of the third week, a miracle happened. My fever disappeared, and my appetite returned. I was ready to hit the road again. From that point on I would not only serve my country with my music, I would also serve God, thanks to Keith. Keith stayed in India, and I caught up with the band. Before I left, I told Keith that I didn't know how I could ever thank him for what he'd done for me. We said good-bye, and I never saw Chaplain Keith again.

I'm retired from the Army now, but certainly not from my bugle. I'm called on regularly to sound "Taps" at military events and funerals. I feel honored to continue serving my country by paying a musical tribute to the soldiers who have gone on before me. But on one such occasion, the 24 notes of "Taps" took on a deeper meaning to me than they ever had before.

It was September 14, 2001, just three days after the attacks on the World Trade Center. A bugler friend of mine called me to sub for him at the last minute to sound "Taps" at a funeral for a casualty of those attacks. I took down the time and location, but in my rush, I didn't get the name. I showed up and introduced myself to the family standing next to a flag-draped casket. Then a glance at a photo of the deceased stopped me cold.

It was Keith—the Army chaplain I'd met in India. Apparently he had been ministering to some victims as a volunteer and was hit by some debris from an explosion. I swallowed hard, not knowing if I could carry through with my task. But I knew I had to—I owed it to Keith. I steered clear of people until that part of the ceremony for which I was summoned. I didn't want to stir up any more emotion, so I silently prayed for strength to continue. The moment came, and every single note became a prayer for Keith. By the grace of God, I made it through without faltering. This experience reminded me of the invocation delivered by retired Chaplain (Colonel) Edward Brogan of the United States Air Force at the "Taps" Exhibit Opening Ceremony at Arlington National Cemetery in 1999:

*(**Optional:** Actor may read from a written prayer)*

"Lord of our lives, our hope in death, we cannot listen to 'Taps' without our souls stirring. Its plaintive notes are a prayer in music—of hope, of peace, of grief, of rest . . . Prepare us too, Lord, for our final bugle call when you summon us home! When the trumpet of the Lord shall sound and death will be no more."

(SEAN *salutes the American flag, exits.)*

Puppet Script

Our Country

by Wanda E. Brunstetter

Puppet Characters:

DONNIE
SUSAN

SUSAN *(enters, appears to be looking for something)*: Hmm . . . now where did I put that history book?

DONNIE *(enters)*: Hi, Susan. What are you up to?

SUSAN: Columbus Day is coming soon and I wanted to read the story of Christopher Columbus, but I can't find my history book.

DONNIE *(singing)*: Columbus sailed the ocean blue, in 1492 . . . I wonder if his boat looked like a floating zoo.

SUSAN: No, Donnie, you're thinking of Noah's boat. That's the one with the floating zoo.

DONNIE: You mean Noah sailed his ark in 1492?

SUSAN: No, no. Columbus sailed in 1492.

DONNIE: But you just said it was Noah.

SUSAN *(exasperated)*: I said Noah had a floating zoo.

DONNIE: In 1492?

SUSAN: No. Noah lived on earth way before that. It was in the early Bible days. Remember when we learned that story in Sunday School a few weeks ago?

DONNIE: Oh yeah. Wasn't that the one about how God flooded the earth because men were so sinful?

SUSAN: That's right, and since Noah was the only righteous man, God told him to build a big boat and to take his whole family on board. He also told him to take two of every animal, as well as some others they would need for food. God instructed them to stay on the boat until the waters receded and He said it was time to get off.

DONNIE: I'm sure glad I didn't have to ride on that boat. Just think of all those smelly animals. Phew! *(Looking right at* SUSAN.*)* Say, did Columbus have lots of animals on his boat too?

SUSAN: I doubt it, Donnie. I'm sure he had sailors, though. They sailed all the way from Spain to America, and that's a long way, so they needed plenty of men to help out.

DONNIE: The calendar on my bedroom wall shows that Columbus Day is a holiday. Why would we celebrate a man with a bunch of sailors on a boat?

SUSAN: Columbus Day is a time we remember Christopher Columbus and are thankful he discovered the wonderful country we live in.

DONNIE *(singing)*: America, America, the trees that shed leaves on me . . . And crown my head with nuts and cones, from fir and maple trees.

SUSAN: That's not how the song goes, silly.

DONNIE: How does it go then?

SUSAN *(singing)*: America, America, God shed His grace on thee . . . And crown thy good with brotherhood, from sea to shining sea.

DONNIE: I did have some of the words right.

SUSAN: There's also a song called, "God Bless America," and another one entitled, "My Country 'Tis of Thee." Songs like those remind us that we live in a great country where every man and woman is free.

DONNIE: So, getting back to Christopher Columbus . . . if he hadn't discovered America, we might not be living here now, right?

SUSAN: That's right, Donnie.

DONNIE: Wow, I feel so proud to be an American.

SUSAN: Me too. Shall we invite the audience to sing "America the Beautiful" with us?

DONNIE: Sure. *(To audience.)* Won't you join me and Susan as we sing the first and last verse of "America the Beautiful"?

(When song is over, both puppets say: "Happy Columbus Day," and exit.)

Short Scripts

Remembering Someone Special

by Margaret Primrose

Cast:

MOTHER
JOEL
ANDREA

JOEL: Mom, do we have to go to the cemetery again this year?

MOTHER: Well, there's no law that forces us to do it, but I always like to decorate Joey's grave on Memorial Day.

ANDREA: He never sees the flowers we leave there.

MOTHER: That's true, but it helps me to remember him and to thank the Lord for the few short years we had him with us.

JOEL: I don't think he cared much about flowers.

MOTHER: Oh, I think everyone enjoys flowers.

JOEL: Maybe, but I'd rather leave a toy than a bunch of daises or lilacs.

ANDREA: So would I.

MOTHER: What kind of toy do you have in mind?

JOEL: He liked pinwheels.

ANDREA: That's right, he did. I could use some of my allowance to buy one.

JOEL: I've already spent my allowance.

MOTHER: That's not a big problem. A pinwheel is easy to make with a pencil, a pin, and a piece of heavy paper. You could draw a picture on your pinwheels before I teach you how to put them together.

ANDREA: Why not?

MOTHER: Don't forget, there's something we always do before we leave the cemetery.

ANDREA: We won't forget. We'll talk about the funny things he did and said. Then we'll bow our heads and thank God for him.

JOEL: Mom, will you and Daddy let me take Bobby with us?

MOTHER: Why not?

ANDREA: I want to take Allison too.

MOTHER: Very good. I'd especially like to tell them about the night Joey prayed for Jesus to be his Savior.

A Soldier's Mother

by Rebecca K. Grosenbach

Cast:

REVOLUTIONARY WAR MOTHER
CIVIL WAR MOTHER
WORLD WAR I MOTHER
WORLD WAR II MOTHER
KOREAN WAR MOTHER
VIETNAM WAR MOTHER
MIDDLE EAST WAR MOTHER

Props:

A large table, perhaps some baskets
A few chairs if desired for variety in staging
A large pile of clean clothes, pieces of fabric, towels

Costumes: Each MOTHER should be dressed in a way that will identify her time period.

Production Note: Each MOTHER should fold clothing or items that would have been around during her time period. As each enters, she will join the previous MOTHER in folding items. She should be in place before beginning her lines. Change the timing of the entrances as necessary so the women don't have to hurry. It would also be helpful to use slides of each specific time period to help set the tone.

(Lights come up with REVOLUTIONARY WAR MOTHER *standing at table folding time appropriate clothes.)*

REVOLUTIONARY WAR MOTHER: I never believed it would come to this. We are at war. Fighting against England. And to think we used to pledge our allegiance to the King! How was it phrased in the great Declaration? ". . . He has plundered our Seas, ravaged our Coasts, burnt our towns, and destroyed the Lives of our People."

*(*CIVIL WAR MOTHER *enters.)*

So we have proclaimed our Independence and now we're killing and being killed to make it a reality. Husbands, sons, left home to stand together to make us a free land.

REVOLUTIONARY & CIVIL WAR MOTHERS: It's necessary, I suppose . . .

CIVIL WAR MOTHER: I believed we could settle our differences without guns, without killing. But now, brother fighting against brother, cousin against cousin, my own son, off to war. North, South, slave, free, old men, young men—

(WW I MOTHER enters.)

REVOLUTIONARY & CIVIL WAR MOTHERS: They're all willing to die for what they believe.

CIVIL WAR MOTHER *(looking up to quote from the Gettysburg Address by Lincoln)*: "Now we are engaged in a great civil war, testing whether that nation, or any nation so conceived and so dedicated, can long endure."

ALL THREE MOTHERS: And our nation shall endure, as long as our boys are willing to defend it.

WW I MOTHER: Willing to defend our own country, far, far from home. President Wilson thought we could stay out of the war in Europe. But he says the United States is threatened now, what with Germany's U-boats. So our boys are over there fighting and dying in places I'll never see. *(Pauses in folding to quote poem)*

We are the Dead. Short days ago
We lived, felt dawn, saw sunset glow,
Loved, and were loved, and now we lie
In Flanders fields.*

(WW II MOTHER enters.)

In far away places our boys give their lives, not just for our freedom, but for the freedom of the whole world.

REVOLUTIONARY, CIVIL, & WW I MOTHERS: I'll admit, I'm afraid I'll never see him again.

REVOLUTIONARY WAR MOTHER: That . . . he'll die.

CIVIL WAR MOTHER: And I'll never . . .

WW II MOTHER: But I mustn't dwell on that. It's right for him to be there. Once Pearl Harbor was bombed how could we not get involved? It was bad enough to hear what was happening in London, in Paris, all over Europe. But when our own ships were attacked we had to respond.

(KOREAN WAR MOTHER enters.)

WW I & WW II MOTHERS: But we have Allies and we'll fight together.

WW I MOTHER: Fight against the advances of evil.

ALL: Our boys are brave and strong. They'll be victorious.

KOREAN WAR MOTHER: They'll win the war. Even though they don't really call it a war. It's a "police action." Well, call it what you will. Boys are dying to defend what is right. Sounds like war to me.

*(*VIETNAM WAR MOTHER *enters.)*

KOREAN WAR MOTHER: They say we need to stop the spread of Communism.

WW II & KOREAN WAR MOTHERS: What happens on the other side of the world affects us too.

WW I MOTHER: So they say.

ALL: I have to believe the cause is just and that my boy will be home soon.

VIETNAM WAR MOTHER: He'll be home soon. And this terrible war will end.

CIVIL & VIETNAM WAR MOTHERS: We're fighting each other . . .

VIETNAM WAR MOTHER: As much as we're fighting the Vietnamese. The papers and TV news are full of protests against the war.

*(*MIDDLE EAST WAR MOTHER *enters.)*

CIVIL & VIETNAM WAR MOTHERS: There's never been such division in our country.

ALL: I pray for him all day, every day.

MIDDLE EAST WAR MOTHER: Pray that he'll be safe, be alert. The battle lines are so unclear. He could be shot just walking down the street.

(Speak the next few lines as one unbroken sentence, other voices joining in as indicated.)

It's not like other wars with . . .

MIDDLE EAST & WW II MOTHERS: soldiers storming up beaches in France . . .

MIDDLE EAST WAR MOTHER: or . . .

MIDDLE EAST & VIETNAM WAR MOTHERS: wading through rice paddies.

MIDDLE EAST WAR MOTHER: It's just so strange.

(All MOTHERS *stop folding clothes and speak as if talking to themselves, not really addressing the audience, just looking out into space.)*

ALL: But freedom comes at a cost.

CIVIL WAR MOTHER: And sometimes the price is the life of someone's son . . .

REVOLUTIONARY & MIDDLE EAST WAR MOTHERS: or father . . .

VIETNAM WAR MOTHER: or brother.

(Pause)

WW I MOTHER: But I'm proud of him.

MIDDLE EAST WAR MOTHER: Proud of all the men and women willing to leave their families for a time.

VIETNAM WAR MOTHER: Even if everyone doesn't agree . . .

KOREAN WAR MOTHER: We can all be proud of those who serve.

WW II MOTHER: And we can all watch and pray.

ALL: Pray that they'll all come home.

MIDDLE EAST WAR MOTHER: Soon . . .

CIVIL WAR MOTHER: And we must resolve, as did President Lincoln,

VIETNAM WAR MOTHER: That these dead shall not have died in vain,

ALL: That this nation under God . . .

REVOLUTIONARY & WW I MOTHERS: shall have a new birth of freedom,

KOREAN WAR MOTHER: and that government of the people,

WW II MOTHER: by the people,

MIDDLE EAST WAR MOTHER: for the people,

ALL: shall not perish from the earth.

(Lights quickly fade to black.)

*"In Flanders Fields," by John McCrae

Program

A Memorial Day Service for Church or School

by Dorothy Heibel

("Fife and Drum Corps" enter to drumbeat pattern and flute melody. Three children are dressed in present-day clothing. One carries the American flag, one plays the drum, and the third plays the flute. Drum and flute perform, "When Johnny Comes Marching Home." The three parade around stage as song is performed twice, stopping to stand in middle of stage, facing audience, at close of song.)

LEADER *(in suit, enters SR):* Will the people please stand. *(Audience stands.)* Let us repeat the Pledge of Allegiance together.

I pledge allegiance to the Flag of the United States of America, and to the Republic for which it stands: one Nation under God, indivisible, with Liberty and Justice for all.

("Fife and Drum Corps" marches offstage to same strains of "When Johnny Comes Marching Home.")

LEADER: You may be seated.

(Boy representing ABE LINCOLN *appears onstage. He is wearing a stovepipe hat and beard.)*

LEADER: Ah, Abe, you did come back today as you promised.

ABE: Yes, dear people. I have come back to the present from the year 1863 when I orated the Gettysburg Address during the Civil War.

LEADER: Of course, Abe. It was a very famous speech, one we'd like to hear again. We will pretend it is November 19th, 1863. We are in Gettysburg, Pennsylvania, once more listening to your speech.

ABE: Very well. Of course, since I wrote it, I did have it memorized once, but after some 142 years, I need a reminder, so I will read the speech.

LEADER: Yes, yes, we understand. Go ahead!

ABE:

Four score and seven years ago our fathers brought forth on this continent, a new nation, conceived in Liberty, and dedicated to the proposition that all men are created equal.

Now we are engaged in a great civil war, testing whether that nation, or any nation so conceived and so dedicated, can long endure. We are met on a great battle-field of that war. We have come to dedicate a portion of that field, as a final resting place for those who here gave their lives that that nation might live. It is altogether fitting and proper that we should do this.

But, in a larger sense, we cannot dedicate—we cannot consecrate—we cannot hallow—this ground. The brave men, living and dead, who struggled here, have consecrated it, far above our poor power to add or detract. The world will little note, nor long remember what we say here, but it can never forget what they did here. It is for us the living, rather, to be dedicated here to the unfinished work which they who fought here have thus far so nobly advanced. It is rather for us to be here dedicated to the great task remaining before us—that from these honored dead we take increased devotion to that cause for which they gave the last full measure of devotion—that we here highly resolve that these dead shall not have died in vain—that this nation, under God, shall have a new birth of freedom—and that government of the people, by the people, for the people, shall not perish from the earth.

LEADER *(leading applause):* Will the people please stand. We thank you, Mr. Lincoln, for this reminder of our past. *(People standing)* Will you now read with me the prayer.

LEADER: Bring down your blessing upon us, O Lord.

PEOPLE: Amen.

LEADER: Bring down your peace upon us, O Lord.

PEOPLE: Amen.

LEADER: Help us to always honor the brave men who have fought for the honor of our country: those who live and those who die.

PEOPLE: Amen.

LEADER: Unto you, Lord, we pray for justice. By your hand may we also attain peace.

PEOPLE: Amen.

LEADER: Peace in our hearts and minds and souls, and peace between nations and races.

PEOPLE: Amen.

LEADER: We honor the soldiers who fought to defend those weaker nations in the name of "liberty and justice for all." As we mourn our fallen heroes may we always remember that they stood for the betterment of mankind and a safer place in which to live.

ALL: Praise God who rules our world!

LEADER: Let us sing, "God Bless America."

(As people sing, bugler enters, plays "Taps" at close of song.)